Fajr and Noor

Collection of Meaningful Quotes.

Written by s.hukr

Fajr and Noor

Publisher: Fajr Noor © 2024

All Rights Reserved

ISBN: 9780645766639

Designed & Authored by s.hukr

Website: fajrnoor.com

Fajr and Noor

Salam.

I hope you find peace, wisdom, and love through these words. I hope this book inspires you to love yourself, educate yourself and become a better Muslim.

May Allah guide you toward that which is best while making your Dunya and your Deen easy for you.

If there is a word that you do not understand, simply search the definition of the word on Google.com.

e.g. "Define [word]"

fajrnoor.com

Fajr and Noor

If you lie, you are a coward.

If you're a man without
responsibilities, you're still a boy.

If you think money will
make you happy, you're a fool.

If you fear death, you aren't
ready to meet your lord.

s.hukr

Fajr and Noor

Death remembered you,
but did you remember death?

s.hukr

Fajr and Noor

Praying five times is not optional,
it is compulsory, it is a duty, it is peace.

You are accountable and
you will be held responsible.

s.hukr

Fajr and Noor

We are not angels, but when we walk
towards righteousness, only then we
become better than angels.

s.hukr

Fajr and Noor

God is so faithful that He will wreck
your plans before they wreck you.

s.hukr

Fajr and Noor

Everyday establish a relationship
with the Quran. Read, memorise,
understand, recite, and study the
words of your lord.

Whether it be a few lines every day
or a complete juz or tafseer.

Do not sleep until you have
maintained a relationship with
God's words.

s.hukr

Fajr and Noor

Shukr is when you look
at the poor, not at the rich.

s.hukr

Fajr and Noor

We are often ready to impress our friends
and family with our wealth by flexing brands
like Gucci, LV and Rolex but when will we
please the Almighty by giving charity?

s.hukr

Fajr and Noor

The quality of blessing is in shukr. The more you are grateful, the more your blessings increase.

s.hukr

Fajr and Noor

When you truly love Islam, you
adorn yourself with the sunnah,
you admire the prophet and
are eager to meet your lord.

s.hukr

Fajr and Noor

A woman in Islam is treated
like a queen, nothing less.

s.hukr

Fajr and Noor

You can have the materialistic things,
the girls and the devil's whispers.

But I want Allah, my queen and
to leave a real purpose before I depart.

s.hukr

Fajr and Noor

Your mind will believe
everything you tell it.

Feed it faith, feed it truth,
feed it the love of Islam.

s.hukr

Fajr and Noor

My love for this world is as temporary
as this world is to me. But my love for
you is eternal, just as you are to me.

s.hukr

Fajr and Noor

This halal haram ratio shouldn't be
normalised. You can't hold hands with
Allah and Shaytan at the same time.

s.hukr

Fajr and Noor

Filters and makeup make you look
picture perfect, but I wanna fall in
love with your imperfections.

s.hukr

Fajr and Noor

The angels are perfect yet Allah still
made them inferior to us.

Ever wondered why?

s.hukr

Fajr and Noor

When we have important decisions to make in life. We should firstly seek the guidance of Allah because He knows what is the absolute best for us.

s.hukr

Fajr and Noor

Fajr:

The whole world sleeps except
for lovers who stay awake
telling stories to God.

s.hukr

Fajr and Noor

It wasn't meant to be.
You're not missing out.

Allah has different plans for you.

s.hukr

Fajr and Noor

The life of this world starts to become boring every time I start to read about Paradise.

s.hukr

Fajr and Noor

Allah turns night into the day, what
makes you think He can't turn
hardship into happiness?

s.hukr

Fajr and Noor

You pursue the delights of this world,
trying to attain the glamorous perfections
we all see and hear. But forget about the
condition your soul, whom will enter the
grave and will be questioned about **Faith**.

s.hukr

Fajr and Noor

If a Man can't lead you in **Salah**,
How can he lead you in Life?

s.hukr

Fajr and Noor

Boys who treat their mothers
and sisters the best, will make
the best husbands.

s.hukr

Fajr and Noor

The answer to your
Dua is never late.

It is always on time.

s.hukr

Fajr and Noor

Allah without man is still Allah,
but a man without Allah is nothing.

s.hukr

Fajr and Noor

In the veil I am seen,
but without it I am hidden.

s.hukr

Fajr and Noor

My heart may get dirty every day
but I repent every night.

s.hukr

Fajr and Noor

I am human. I am weak.
I am far from perfect.
I make mistakes.

But as long as I stay
sincere with God,
my destination will
remain in Paradise.

s.hukr

Fajr and Noor

If you have Allah, how can
you ever feel alone?

s.hukr

Fajr and Noor

Regret eats you up, a punishment
from yourself.

Forgive yourself, before you
ruin yourself.

s.hukr

Fajr and Noor

If he can't maintain a
relationship with Allah,

how will he maintain a
relationship with you?

s.hukr

Fajr and Noor

Treat your parents with kindness and love,
your children will watch and learn,
and treat you the same.

s.hukr

Fajr and Noor

Those that do not want **Jannah**.

Let them sleep, only Allah can help
them. But don't forget to mention
their name in your Duas.

s.hukr

Fajr and Noor

Every single human to walk this earth
has the potential to attain **Jannah**.
Some just never try.

s.hukr

Fajr and Noor

Some love me,
Some hate me.

Who cares?
Allah is with me.

s.hukr

Fajr and Noor

Gems keep themselves hidden,
they are pure, priceless,
and beautiful.

You are the gem.

s.hukr

Fajr and Noor

Treat everyone with respect and dignity despite the differences in culture, religion, race, or gender.

We are all humans at the end of the day.

s.hukr

Fajr and Noor

You have eyes but you are blind.
Learn to see with your heart.

s.hukr

Fajr and Noor

Don't worry about going left or right,
up or down, just keep walking,
keep trying your best.

At the end of each day,
ask for Allah's guidance
and keep walking.

s.hukr

Fajr and Noor

Islam tells us to assume the
best in people yet we judge
quicker than a blink of
an eye.

Why do we do that?

s.hukr

Fajr and Noor

The solution to our problems was
introduced to us **1400 years ago**,
however our culture tends to leave it
on the bookshelf collecting dust,
rather than understanding it and
applying it.

s.hukr

Fajr and Noor

Hate what is wrong, but don't
hate the one who errors.

Criticise speech but respect
the speaker. Kill the disease,
not the patient.

s.hukr

Fajr and Noor

While everyone wishes to
become a king or queen,
the king of all kings
awaits for our call.

s.hukr

Fajr and Noor

Women who call men trash,
they are equally as **trash**.

s.hukr

Fajr and Noor

How foolish have you become to leave
your Salah for this temporary Dunya?

Get up, I can't bear to see you harm yourself.
Get up, make wudu, I'm waiting for you…

s.hukr

Fajr and Noor

My wife probably out there praying Fajr alone
and thinking about staying single for life.

Sorry boo, Allah made us in pairs.

s.hukr

Fajr and Noor

Being humble is so attractive.
I love people that do a lot and
don't speak a word.

People that just let their actions
speak for them and are laid back.
They are my favourite type of people.

s.hukr

Fajr and Noor

I'm not on the left side or the right.

I'm in the middle, I follow **Islam**,
trying to follow the straight path.

s.hukr

Fajr and Noor

My future wife probably thinks she's going to
marry some financially stable king.

Sorry boo, I just got fired, don't yell at me.

s.hukr

Fajr and Noor

To some, **Islam** is nothing but
rules and regulations, halal and
haram.

But to those who understand,
it is a perfect vision of life,
a straight path that leads
to paradise.

s.hukr

Fajr and Noor

The real problem isn't religion.

Rather it is the lack of knowledge
or the lack of application of that
knowledge that **oppresses**.

s.hukr

Fajr and Noor

Worries end when you start your day
with Fajr and end your day with Isha.

s.hukr

Fajr and Noor

I see men and women competing with
each other. How foolish have you become;
you are not the same.

Rather, you were made to
complement each other.

s.hukr

Fajr and Noor

Muslim boys want to connect their
beard but won't pray Salah.

Bro you worried about the wrong connection.

Muslim girls missing Salah because
they can't do wudu with makeup on.

Sis you worried about the wrong foundation.

s.hukr

Fajr and Noor

The bond between men and women
is the very fabric of society.

The condition of that bond has a direct
correlation with the condition of the
society itself.

s.hukr

Fajr and Noor

Those that love you more than they
love Allah, become blind.

s.hukr

Fajr and Noor

Make a conscious effort
to be Muslim every day.

s.hukr

Fajr and Noor

Men admire me and Women want
to be with me,

but I admire the Prophet's life and
desire an eternity of happiness.

s.hukr

Fajr and Noor

You can't enjoy your wealth
without good health, so do not
neglect your **body** or your **mind**.

Help yourself. If you can't,
seek strength from Allah.

s.hukr

Fajr and Noor

Our Prophet cooked, cleaned, and
took out the trash.

He didn't treat his wives like maids.
He treated them like partners.

Be like Muhammad.

s.hukr

Fajr and Noor

Relationships that consist of
a 'girlfriend' or 'boyfriend'

or are outside the realms
of marriage, they are
forbidden in Islam.

We believe in **Commitment**
and **Honour**.

s.hukr

Fajr and Noor

If prayers remain unanswered, do we ever
reflect that it may be for our own good?

Maybe one day you'll be thankful to Allah
for not giving you every single thing that
you prayed for.

s.hukr

Fajr and Noor

Hijab is for the **body**.
Haya is for the **soul**.

s.hukr

Fajr and Noor

In **Islam,**

Hijab is fard,
Salah is fard,
Zakat is fard.

s.hukr

Fajr and Noor

Never have I ever dealt with anything
more difficult than my own nafs,

which sometimes helps me and
sometimes opposes me.

s.hukr

Fajr and Noor

A True Muslim does not backbite,
create false rumours or thinks ill
about someone.

Rather he treats everyone with respect,
dignity and assumes the best in people,
no matter the colour of their skin,
their religion or gender.

s.hukr

Fajr and Noor

Learn to control your desires,
do not let your desires control you.

Be the **master** to your soul,
not the **slave**.

s.hukr

Fajr and Noor

Not everybody deserves to
see your personality.

Let them think your dry.
Who cares?

s.hukr

Fajr and Noor

To all my brothers struggling
to grow a beard, have hope bro.

If aunties can do it, so can you.

s.hukr

Fajr and Noor

A brothers love always protects you.

A sisters love always follows you.

s.hukr

Fajr and Noor

You glow differently when
you start your day with **Fajr**.

s.hukr

Fajr and Noor

Ramadan, I miss you.

s.hukr

Fajr and Noor

Just because someone does wrong,
doesn't mean you do another wrong.

s.hukr

Fajr and Noor

Life is like a bitter cup of tea.
Iman, **Salah** & **Sabr** are the
sugar cubes.

The spoon is in your hand.
You control the **sweetness**.

s.hukr

Fajr and Noor

Being **Muslim** is not a label,
it is a **responsibility**.

Islam is not just a religion,
it is a **lifestyle**.

Quran not just a book,
it is **God's message** to mankind.

s.hukr

Fajr and Noor

Sadness that brings you back to Allah
is better than happiness that
takes you from him.

s.hukr

Fajr and Noor

Who are you to expose someone,
while Allah keeps their sins hidden?

s.hukr

Fajr and Noor

I was born in the west,
but the **Adhan** is what made
me fall in love with the east.

s.hukr

Fajr and Noor

Don't wait for someone to
bring you flowers.

Plant your own garden and
decorate your own soul.

s.hukr

Fajr and Noor

You must learn to love Allah first,
before you learn to love me.

s.hukr

Fajr and Noor

She Exists.

She is ambitious but humble.
She is educated and open minded.
She doesn't gossip or backbite.
She doesn't go out with boys.
She doesn't call men trash,
She is modest and pure.

She is a **Queen**.
Yes, She Exists.

s.hukr

Fajr and Noor

As long as you have Allah,
you will never feel alone.

The angels will always
keep you company.

s.hukr

Fajr and Noor

The Prophet lived a simple life.
He was not poor, his heart was the
richest amongst us all.

s.hukr

Fajr and Noor

Love yourself enough to know that
you will enter paradise. But beware,
too much self-love will make you selfish.

s.hukr

Fajr and Noor

Stop worrying about things
beyond your control.

Make Dua and leave
the rest to Allah.

"Tie the camel and then
trust in His plan."

s.hukr

Fajr and Noor

The first bond between mankind
was marriage, between man and
woman, it was inscribed by Allah.

s.hukr

Fajr and Noor

Do not force Islam upon your family.
Rather show them the beauty of Islam
through your actions.

s.hukr

Fajr and Noor

Some of us stay up late entertaining the devil,
And some of us stay up late talking to God.

Which one are you?

s.hukr

Fajr and Noor

Remind yourself, that if God sent
everyone away from you, it is so that
you could spend more time with him.

s.hukr

Fajr and Noor

My safe place is **Fajr**.

The world sleeps except
for you and me.

s.hukr

Fajr and Noor

When a person draws closer to Allah and becomes more righteous, they also become wiser and more peaceful. They become calm, kind and composed.

People begin to describe them as an "old soul". And that is true, because they're returning back to their original soul.

The soul that stood in front of Allah in another realm, a long time ago and said, **"Yes I believe"**.

s.hukr

Fajr and Noor

Tell me!

How can you feel alone when
you have Allah closer to you
than your jugular vein?

s.hukr

Fajr and Noor

Love exists.
So do lovers.

But most of us are not fortunate
enough to be with our soulmates.

Being in love for a lifetime is a luxury
money can never buy.

s.hukr

Fajr and Noor

Everything awaits its time. Neither the rose blooms before it's time, nor does the sun rise before its time.

Sabr, what is yours will find you!

s.hukr

Fajr and Noor

Don't hold back compliments!

It could make someone's day,
while you earn the good deed.

s.hukr

Fajr and Noor

**Every man is a male,
but not every male is a man.**

Many are still boys who have
yet to reach manhood.

Real men do not fear death,
they are warriors through
every hardship they face.

They do not let anger and
rage consume them.

They are fit to be leaders,
they bear knowledge within them.

They carry tongues sweet enough
to melt a city of gold and their hearts
are strong enough to carry a mountain of gold.

They are righteous men who
live for the hereafter not for this Dunya.

s.hukr

Fajr and Noor

I love calm and gentle personas.

No need to show off, just be yourself.
Someone close to Allah. No envy, no
weird type of jealousy.

You do you and I'll do me while
appreciating the fact that we can
always go back to one another.

s.hukr

Fajr and Noor

Capturing a women's heart is easy when
your tongue is as sweet as honey, more
fragrant than musk and warm enough
to ignite a flame in her heart.

Just be sure that the flame **never** dies.

s.hukr

Fajr and Noor

Idk who needs to hear this but
five times Salah doesn't make
you religious, it makes you Muslim.

s.hukr

Fajr and Noor

There are people who have wealth
but cannot buy a good night sleep,
who cannot buy true love or happiness.

There are people who look so beautiful yet
their insecurities eat them up behind closed
doors.

There are people who have worldly success,
yet have no time to spend with their children,
their spouse or parents.

Say **Alhamdulillah** and feel grateful for
all that you have and do not complain.

But if you are pious and righteous,
and submit yourself towards Deen,
then you have attained success in
Dunya and Akhirah.

s.hukr

Fajr and Noor

If everything you liked was halal,
then how would life be a test?
s.hukr

Fajr and Noor

Help others, so you can help yourself
through the good deeds you earn.

s.hukr

Fajr and Noor

Stop showing off and
comparing yourself
to others.

Be grateful for the
simple things in life,
like the food that you have,
the shelter that protects,
the good health that you
have been given.

Be Grateful and Thank God.

Because if He wanted too,
He could take it away
within a heartbeat.

s.hukr

Fajr and Noor

Islam tells us to assume
the best in people,
so why do you assume
the worst in others?

s.hukr

Fajr and Noor

Allah made women more
beautiful than men.

That's why she must **cover**
herself and why he should
lower his **gaze**.

s.hukr

Fajr and Noor

Iqra!
Seeking knowledge has been
made compulsory for all Muslims.

s.hukr

Fajr and Noor

Stop smoking shisha and blowing
smoke into your camera.

It's not attractive telling people
you might get lung cancer.

s.hukr

Fajr and Noor

People who pray Fajr then go for
a morning walk/jog have their
lives together.

s.hukr

Fajr and Noor

There is nothing wrong to marry
a divorced woman.

There is nothing wrong to
marry an older woman.

Actually, it's the **sunnah**,
the Prophet did it.

s.hukr

Fajr and Noor

The eyes are very beautiful such they allow
you to see. We take it for granted, to see so
many beautiful colours.

Contrast, Highlights, Lighting, Shadows,
Depth, Details are all calculated at such high
precision and in such high quality,
SubhanAllah.

They are very special and are a blessing from
Allah. Use them to see good as they have a
direct relationship with the heart and soul,
don't abuse them.

There is reason why we lower our gaze.
There is wisdom behind that.

s.hukr

Fajr and Noor

Did you remember **Death** today?
Did you say **Alhamdulilah** today?
Did you remember **Allah**?

s.hukr

Fajr and Noor

There is beauty in every race,
brown, black, white, no matter
the hue, in God's eyes we are all equal,
except those who are righteous,
for they are closer and more
beloved to God.

s.hukr

Fajr and Noor

It's always the humble people
that my heart gets along with.

s.hukr

Fajr and Noor

Some are afraid of heights and
others afraid of depth.

Learn to fear Allah alone and watch
how he raises you above mountains.

s.hukr

Fajr and Noor

Nobody is perfect.
Nobody will be perfect.

But that doesn't stop you from
walking towards perfection.
Walking towards Jannah.

s.hukr

Fajr and Noor

Mother.
God made Jannah lie under her feet,
imagine the love that lies in her heart.

s.hukr

Fajr and Noor

Salah is the solution to all your problems and **Dua** is how you communicate with the All Mighty.

s.hukr

Fajr and Noor

You are a hidden gem worth more than gold,
musk and pearls, I would give you my heart
but you already took it.

s.hukr

Fajr and Noor

Idk about you but a girl who wears hijab
for the sake of Allah and a guy who keeps
a beard for the sake of Allah, they become
Hella attractive.

God puts **Noor** on their faces.

s.hukr

Fajr and Noor

A mosque is like a country's capital,
it is the heart of a Muslim society.

s.hukr

Fajr and Noor

My mother, who taught me faith by her love
and manners through her actions.

I am forever in debt to you.

s.hukr

Fajr and Noor

Everything is temporary.
So where are you going?

s.hukr

Fajr and Noor

Islam doesn't forbid a girl
from leaving the house.

It just requires her to be
accompanied by a bodyguard (mahram)
because that's how precious she is.

s.hukr

Fajr and Noor

Treat people with so much respect
and kindness that they can't imagine
Jannah without you.

s.hukr

A Turkish Love Story

Her: How do you like your coffee?
Him: Salty.

s.hukr

Fajr and Noor

Our parents were patient
when we were young.

Now it is our turn to
be patient with them.

s.hukr

Fajr and Noor

If you can't make her laugh or smile,
how will you keep her **happy**?

s.hukr

Fajr and Noor

Self-love is not an excuse to be **selfish**.

Your personal bubble is important but that
doesn't mean you have total disregard for the
public and private rights of others.

Avoid selfishness, desire for your brother,
what you desire for yourself.

s.hukr

Fajr and Noor

Your fate has been written with the ink
of His love and sealed with His mercy.

You are exactly where He wants you to be.
So fear not, place your trust in Him and
have hope in His plan.

s.hukr

Fajr and Noor

The best moments of my life
don't make it to social media.

s.hukr

Fajr and Noor

You a strong man when anger
boils your blood but you remain
silent and in full control.

s.hukr

Fajr and Noor

The idea of marriage is so beautiful like
you live life with the one person you can
trust the most, someone who is always there
for you through thick n thin, you fall in love
countless times.

A best friend, no, your soul mate who
completes half your Deen and becomes
the source of blessings and happiness for
you in this life and in the next.

s.hukr

Fajr and Noor

If you ever see a happy person, promise
me that you won't get jealous, just rejoice,
be happy for them.

Only God knows if that person
may have cried before it.

s.hukr

Fajr and Noor

Never allow someone's opinion
to take away your peace,
even if it is your own family.

s.hukr

Fajr and Noor

A Brown Love Story

Her: I like your beard.
Him: I like yours too.

s.hukr

Fajr and Noor

If this ummah was actually united,
we could conquer the 7 continents.

s.hukr

Fajr and Noor

Islam is not a religion where you pick
and choose what you want and leave
out what you do not want.

Islam is a complete package.

You must acknowledge all of it,
and do your best to follow all the
teachings of Islam.

s.hukr

Fajr and Noor

There is a palace in heaven for every
human who ever walked this earth,
but many will be empty because
they loved the immediate.

s.hukr

Fajr and Noor

While you're busy listening
to the devil's music.

I'm busy falling in love
with God's book.

s.hukr

Fajr and Noor

Stop feeding yourself negative thoughts,
stop overthinking, stop thinking
about the past.

Focus on the present.

Love yourself enough to know
that you will enter paradise.

s.hukr

Fajr and Noor

Allah indirectly tells us:

Stop overthinking, Stop complaining,
Stop stressing yourself too much.
Instead, you should trust me,
Where is your trust in me?

I love you more than you can
imagine, I won't let you down.
That's all you need to know.

s.hukr

Fajr and Noor

Invest so much time, love, and effort in
yourself, that people would love to meet you.
You inspire them just being around them.

They love the beauty hidden in your eyes
because it's the soul that speaks volume.

s.hukr

Fajr and Noor

If you love that which Allah loves,
than how will Allah not grant you
that which you love?

s.hukr

Fajr and Noor

Be sincere with yourself because
God is always watching.

s.hukr

Fajr and Noor

You can meet someone tomorrow
who has better intentions for you
than someone you've known for years,
time means nothing; character does.

s.hukr

Fajr and Noor

Your nose is the right shape.
Your skin is the right shade.
Your lips, hands, feet are the right size.
Your height is perfect and
so is your natural hair colour.
Your voice is beautiful especially
when you laugh.

Whatever you dislike about your
physical self is all in your mind.

Allah created you and
He doesn't make mistakes.
Let that sink in.

s.hukr

Fajr and Noor

I hope someone told you
that you are more valuable
than saffron, musk and gold.

And when you smile,
your face glows with Noor,
your eyes sparkle like stars in the sky
and your smile reminds me of Jannah.

s.hukr

Fajr and Noor

Isn't it embarrassing that
you know lyrics to 100 songs
but repeat the same surahs
in your salah?

s.hukr

Fajr and Noor

If you are Muslim and your opinions
don't align with the Quran and Sunnah,
then please shut your mouth,
I don't want to hear it.

s.hukr

Fajr and Noor

Always assume the best in people
even when things don't seem so.

Treat them how you would like
to be treated.

s.hukr

Fajr and Noor

Sometimes all you need is to close
your eyes and let your soul listen
to the holy Quran.

s.hukr

Fajr and Noor

Brother don't think about
having another wife.

Focus on treating your wife
so well that God lets you
have another one.

s.hukr

Fajr and Noor

Men who are best to their wives,
are entrusted with another by Allah.

And who is foolish enough to oppose Allah?

s.hukr

Fajr and Noor

A pious woman helps bring
up a pious ummah and a
cursed woman will bring
up an unfortunate generation.

This is how important women
are in the world.

s.hukr

Fajr and Noor

Do not entertain the foolish.
Do not add fuel to the fire.

Remain calm and silent,
the flame will burn out
eventually.

s.hukr

Fajr and Noor

Some of us desire the best this Dunya,
but the rest of us desire the best in
the hereafter.

s.hukr

Fajr and Noor

Salam, how are you?

I hope you are well. I just wanted to tell you
that you are beautiful, not because of your skin
care routine, but because you started praying 5
times.

I see Noor glowing from your face because of
wudu. Your soul is happy, content and your
eyes are full of life. I noticed that you also fast
Mondays and Thursdays. I like how you take
care of your body.

You stopped smoking, you're eating healthier,
you started investing time into yourself, I can
tell. May Allah bless you.

I like how you don't argue anymore, been
reading books aye? Knowledge is a beautiful
asset. May Allah increase it. I see love
overflowing from you.

I am happy you changed.

s.hukr

Fajr and Noor

I look forward to meeting
you in Jannah. Insha'Allah.

s.hukr

Fajr and Noor

She isn't looking for someone with a good
pickup line. She wants a man with good
character, a kind & loving heart. Someone
with soft words for her.

A man who respects his womenfolk, who is
loyal. A man who will give her attention, time,
and love.

A man she admires… funny, romantic but also
hardworking and mature.

A man who can control his anger and lust. A
man who she can trust. Someone she wants to
be with in Dunya and Jannah.

She is not so hard to understand.
She just wants pure love.

s.hukr

Fajr and Noor

Sometimes I ponder how
there are people better than
me in status, wealth, and beauty
yet they still complain...

s.hukr

Fajr and Noor

At most Muslim weddings,
the only halal thing is the meat.

And people wonder why there isn't
any Barakat in the marriage?

s.hukr

Fajr and Noor

Sorry, I can't trust a tongue
that finds it so easy to lie.

s.hukr

Fajr and Noor

Be the shoulder they rest their heads on.
Be the sugar they are missing in their tea.
Be the person they want to be with.
Give.... and Allah will give you more.

s.hukr

Fajr and Noor

Islam has taught us that we treat our women
with honour and respect. Allah raised the
status of Women in Islam 1400 years ago.

Who the hell are you to degrade,
disrespect and dishonour them?

s.hukr

Fajr and Noor

As far as the Quran is concerned, sects don't exist in Islam. We are one ummah. We are Muslims. Nothing more, nothing less.

s.hukr

Fajr and Noor

Open your eyes, look within.
Are you satisfied with the
life you're living?

s.hukr

Fajr and Noor

Common sense is not so
common in common people.

s.hukr

Fajr and Noor

People love you because of temporary
things like your beauty, your wealth
and your success, but people love
me because of my heart, my
tongue and my words.

Which one is better?

s.hukr

Fajr and Noor

A real man knows,

How to cook
How to clean
How to love
How to lower his gaze
How to respect women

s.hukr

Fajr and Noor

Some people look forward to hardship,
because they know ease will come
eventually.

s.hukr

Fajr and Noor

Take your broken heart to Thajjud
and reveal it to God, the one
who mends the heart.

s.hukr

Fajr and Noor

If Allah didn't love you,
He would never let you fast
the days of Ramadan and
let you stand its nights.

He gifted you this because
He wanted to forgive you.

s.hukr

Fajr and Noor

As a human, we can't fully understand
the wisdom behind Allah's plans.

So if you gain something, embrace it.
And if you lose something, let it be.
You don't always love what is best for you,
and you don't always hate what is terribly
wrong for you.

Trust in Allah, He knows that which is best.

s.hukr

Fajr and Noor

Nothing moves my soul
like the words of Allah.

s.hukr

Fajr and Noor

Haram is still **Haram,**

even if the whole
world is doing it.

s.hukr

Fajr and Noor

Salam...

Did anyone tell you,
that you look beautiful today?

Well, you look beautiful, especially today.
You deserve to know that.

s.hukr

Fajr and Noor

Sabr is more than patience…
It's about accepting your situation
and knowing that with every hardship
ease will follow.

s.hukr

Fajr and Noor

Extinguish the flame of hatred from
your heart by forgiving everyone
whoever wronged you.

Not for their sake, but in the hope
that Allah will show you mercy.

s.hukr

Fajr and Noor

Allah doesn't need our Salah,
but we are always in need of Allah.

s.hukr

Fajr and Noor

When people test your Sabr,
gnaw off your peace.
Don't argue.
Don't spit venom.

Simply do not care...
There is a ferocity in being unphased,

that people do not understand...
You will remain at peace I assure you.

s.hukr

Fajr and Noor

It's better to have no friends than
to have friends that make you miss Salah.

s.hukr

Fajr and Noor

I let go of so many friends,
just to be closer to Paradise.

s.hukr

Fajr and Noor

Strange, how you chase Dunya
when it was meant as a test for Adam.

s.hukr

Fajr and Noor

I have nothing against 'bad' people
because through them I may benefit,
or they benefit through me.

There will always be good and
bad people, but I rather surround
myself with Allah foremost who
protect me from harm and
guides me closer to goodness.

Because, sometimes it's the 'good'
people that hurt you the most.

s.hukr

Fajr and Noor

It is said that the parents should play with
their children until the age of seven,
teach them for the next seven years,
and after that, be their friends.

s.hukr

Fajr and Noor

If Jannah is your dream,
then hold on to your Deen.

Don't let Shaytan get to you.

s.hukr

Fajr and Noor

A women's true beauty isn't
her figure or features, if only
men knew how to see with
their hearts and not their eyes.

They would notice her **Iman**,
her **Modesty** and her **Loyalty**.

s.hukr

Fajr and Noor

A sign of a beautiful person is that
he always see's the beauty in others.

s.hukr

Fajr and Noor

How dare you expose someone
while Allah keeps their sins hidden.

Who do you think you are?

s.hukr

Fajr and Noor

Righteous men carry tongues
overflowing with love for
their Queens.

s.hukr

Fajr and Noor

My eyes are not blind but
I cannot see, for my heart
is blind and my love is too
great.

s.hukr

Fajr and Noor

In the modern world.
Peace is a luxury many cannot afford.

s.hukr

Fajr and Noor

Most people seem to travel to
places where everyone is
expected to travel.

But one should travel to
where nobody expects.

Explore the unexplored.
Travel to seek God,
not to seek people.

s.hukr

Sad Reality:

Some men find women hard to understand. Even though Allah sent a whole chapter about them. **Surah Al-Nisa**.

s.hukr

Fajr and Noor

Discipline yourself before you
discipline your children.

s.hukr

Fajr and Noor

That haram relationship,
that cursing tongue,
that gossiping mentality,
that materialistic love,
that disrespectful attitude,
that lustful gaze,
that greedy appetite,
that neglected Salah,
that dirty pride
are not befitting a true Believer.

Where is your Salah?
Your fasting? Your Quran?
Your manners? Your honour?
Your good intentions?
Your attractive modesty?
Your kind tongue? Your humbleness?
Your sincere love? Your grateful heart?
Your love for Deen? Your generous smile?
Your charming character?

Oh Muslim, where are you?

s.hukr

Fajr and Noor

Don't let your love towards someone
be more than your love towards Allah.

Sometimes when you love someone too
much, He will take them away from you,
just to see who you love the most.

s.hukr

Fajr and Noor

Know that your time is precious.

Spend it wisely on yourself, so you
can spend an eternity in Paradise.

s.hukr

Fajr and Noor

I encourage every young person to spend time with the Quran and understand it.

If you really understand it, you would practice it for the sole purpose of Allah's pleasure and not for anything in return.

s.hukr

Fajr and Noor

People with a young heart and an
old soul love the deepest.

s.hukr

Fajr and Noor

Jobs fill your pocket but
adventures fill your soul.

The wrong ones will tell you;
you are too much.

The right ones will tell you,
you are an adventure.

s.hukr

Fajr and Noor

Thank you for reading this book.

I hope that you enjoyed it and
found some benefit from my words.

May Allah always have mercy on you
and guide you towards the straight
path. **Ameen.**

Sincerely,
s.hukr

*P.S If you love this book, please promote them, and
share it with others and maybe you'll earn a good deed.*

*P.S.S If you liked this book, you should checkout
my other books.*

fajrnoor.com

S.hukr Books

1. Fajr and Noor

2. Through His Eyes

3. Noor upon Noor

4. Slice of Paradise

5. Mumin Mindset

6. How to Marry a Muslim Girl

7. Divine Love

www.ingramcontent.com/pod-product-compliance
Lightning Source LLC
Chambersburg PA
CBHW021953090426
42811CB00001B/2